MACHINES

• HOW THEY WORK •

DAVID BURNIE

STERLING PUBLISHING CO. INC. NEW YORK

Editor: Thomas Keegan
Design: David West Children's Book Design
Illustrators: David Russell, Mike Saunders and Simon Tegg. Subsidiary illustrations by David Burroughs.

Library of Congress
Cataloging-in-Publication Data Available

10 9 8 7 6 5 4 3 2 1

Published 1994 by Sterling Publishing Company, Inc.
387 Park Avenue South, New York, N.Y. 10016
Originally published by Simon & Schuster Young Books under the title *Machines by Design*
© 1993 by Simon & Schuster Young Books
Distributed in Canada by Sterling Publishing
% Canadian Manda Group,
P.O. Box 920, Station U
Toronto, Ontario, Canada M8Z 5P9

Typeset by Goodfellow and Egan Ltd
Printed and bound in Hong Kong

Sterling ISBN 0-8069-0744-4

CONTENTS

WORLD OF MACHINES

It's hard to imagine a world without machines. We rely on them for many things, from cooking meals and moving about to keeping in touch with other people. A machine is a device that is designed to do a particular job. The first machines were "mechanical," meaning that they worked with moving parts. Today, we still use mechanical machines, but we also have others that work with sound, light or electricity. In this book, you can find out what different parts do to make a machine work.

Gears

Gears are wheels with teeth that fit together so that they turn each other around. Gears are important parts of many machines because they can change the direction, speed or force of a movement. The change depends on the relative sizes of the two gears. You can find out more about gears on pages 16-17.

Levers

A lever is something rigid that can pivot on a point (fulcrum). Levers can also change the direction or force of a movement. For more on levers, see pages 8-10.

Screw

Spiral thread

Screw thread

A screw moves into wood with a great forward force, thanks to its gently sloping thread. Many machines use screw threads to increase a force in this way. As you can see on pages 10-11 they make work easier, but they also make it last longer.

Fulcrum

Small gear turns twice as far and fast, but with half the force

Wheels

Many machines have parts that turn around. On pages 12-13 you can see how wheels move things about. On pages 14-15 you can learn what happens when they move fast.

Turning movement

Forward movement

Heating and cooling

If you go for a run, or take some other kind of exercise, your body will warm up. In the same way, machines make heat when they work. As you can find out on pages 24-25 some machines are especially designed to make heat. They do this by burning a fuel or by using electricity, and they pass on the heat to a place where it is needed. Cooling machines are designed to do exactly the opposite. On pages 26-27 you can see how they help heat to flow from one place to another.

Bird soaring

Rising air

Floating and flying

Floating and flying are two ways of moving through a fluid (liquid or gas). On pages 28-31 you can find out what keeps a balloon or a bird in the air, and how a helicopter manages to take off vertically, or even fly backward.

Using sound and light

Sound and light are two different forms of energy. Sound travels through matter, but light can even travel through empty space. On pages 36-39 you can find out about machines that give out sound and light and about ones that take it in, so that it can be stored or converted into something else.

Eyepiece

Target plate

Cassette

Lens

Computers

Computers are the fastest-changing machines today. They work by converting information into pulses of electricity. On pages 42-45 you can find out more about these pulses.

Monitor

Keyboard

Mouse

Computer

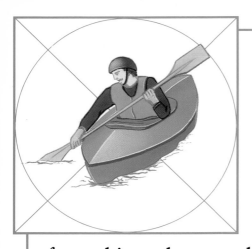

MAKING THINGS MOVE

Whenever you move anything, or change its shape, you have to exert a force. You do this by using your muscles. Machines with moving parts work in a similar way, producing forces by harnessing several different sources of energy. Some machines get their energy from things that are already moving, like air or water. Others obtain energy by releasing it from a fuel or by harnessing electricity. Once something has started to move, it needs a steady supply of energy to keep it going.

FORCE OF WIND

Getting going

To make a skateboard move, you have to exert a force with one of your legs. But you don't push your leg in the direction that you want to go. Instead, you push backward. This action creates

Forward force of reaction

Backward force exerted by leg

a force called reaction that moves the skateboard forward. Reaction appears whenever a force is exerted, and it always pushes in the opposite direction.

Inertia and momentum

It's easy pick up a light object, like a table-tennis ball. But if the ball were filled with lead, you would find it a lot more difficult. This is because the lead-filled ball has a much higher "inertia," which means that it takes much more energy to start or stop. Inertia is important in machines. It means that heavy parts are difficult to set in motion, but once they are moving, they take a long time to slow

Thrust moves board forward

down. An object's "momentum" is a measure of how much energy of movement it has. The two skateboarders shown here have exactly the same momentum.

Heavy object moves more slowly

Light object moves more quickly

Setting sail

A windsurfer harnesses the energy of the wind. If the wind is coming from behind, it presses against the sail and drives the board along. Part of the wind's force may tip the sail over at an angle. The person aboard leans in the other direction to keep the sail upright.

W I N D

Weight of passenger counteracts "heeling force" of wind

Jet engine

A jet engine sucks air with a front fan, then squeezes it into a small space where fuel is burned. The air heats up and suddenly expands, streaming out backward, pushing the engine forward.

Rocket engine

A rocket engine works by the force of reaction. It burns a fuel, and this produces a stream of hot gases, which drives the rocket forward.

Exhaust valve

Inlet valve

Fuel

Piston

Cylinder

Crankshaft

Front fan

Compressor fans

EXHAUST

Fan shaft   Combustion chamber

Running on explosions

A car engine works by making gasoline explode inside a cylinder. The hot gas inside the cylinder expands, and forces the piston out.

Fuel

Liquid oxygen

Combustion chamber

Electric motors

When an electric current flows in a wire, tiny electrons move through it. If the wire is between two magnets, it will move when the current flows. An electric motor has a coil of wires that keeps turning inside a strong magnetic field.

Coil

Magnet

LIGHTENING THE LOAD

Unless you are unusually strong, you will not be able to crack a nut with your bare hands. But with a pair of nutcrackers, the job is easy. They alter the way that the work is done, using levers to magnify the force that you can exert. Many of the devices that we use every day work in this way, trading the force that is exerted for the distance that is moved.

Load

Effort

Fulcrum

Levers in the body
Your lower jaw is a living lever. Like all levers, it rotates around a hinge or a fixed joint called a fulcrum. The back of your jaw is nearest the fulcrum. It travels a small distance, but has a very powerful bite. The front of the jaw travels further, and cannot bite so strongly.

Fulcrum at back of jaw

Force of jaws

Light work
A wheelbarrow makes it easy to lift a heavy object. When you pick up the handles of a wheelbarrow, they move upward much further than the weight. The load is then easily carried between the handles and the fulcrum, which is the wheel of the wheelbarrow.

Force on handles

Jaws

Pressure on object driven by force on handles

Fulcrum

Getting a grip
Pliers use levers to help you apply force to objects more easily. Pliers have long handles and short "jaws." When using the pliers you move the handles a long distance, with little force (or effort). The jaws move a shorter distance, with a much greater force.

Fulcrum

Brake blocks

Tire

Spanner

Screw thread

Bolt

Bicycle brakes

Bicycle brakes use a system of levers to press the brake blocks hard against the wheel. Compared with the brake lever, the blocks move only a tiny distance, but they grip the wheel so hard that it slows down. They change some of the bike's energy of movement into heat.

Jaws

Screw thread

In the grip of a vice

A vice uses a very long screw thread to bring two jaws together. It takes many turns of the handle to move the jaws a small way, but they come together with great force. The long handle works like a lever, to give the screw thread a tighter grip. Long screw threads are used in many car jacks, enabling a driver to lift a car alone.

Taking the easy route

The thread on a bolt is like a gentle slope wound into a spiral. A bolt tightens after many turns and moves forward with great force. In the same way, a staircase increases the distance that has to be moved, but reduces the effort.

Handle

Stopping the flow

The water that comes out of a tap is under great pressure. A tap uses a screw thread to counteract the pressure, and control the flow. The thread moves a rubber washer up to let water out or down to shut it off.

Spindle

Water flows out of tap

Rubber washer

11

WHEELS

The wheel was invented over 5,000 years ago. In those days, wheels were not used for moving about. Instead, they were used to spin slabs of clay to be shaped into pots. A potter's wheel turns horizontally and stays in one place. But soon people found that this wheel could also be used upright, to make things roll along. Since then, wheels have become an essential part of many machines. Wheels and bearings work by reducing friction, the force that opposes movement when one object slides over another.

Rolling along

Before wheels were used for moving, people shifted heavy objects on wooden rollers. Rollers reduce friction, but they have to be picked up and moved as the load slides along.

Wheels on the move

The first cartwheels were solid, and very heavy. Spokes were invented about 4,000 years ago.

Losing weight

A bicycle wheel is strong but light. Its spokes pull against the rim and keep it in shape.

Propeller

A propeller turns on an axle, like a wheel. Instead of rolling forward, it turns sideways. Its blades cut through water, and are angled to push the water backward. This produces a reaction—an equal and opposite force—which drives the boat forward.

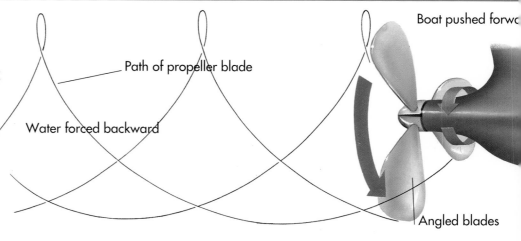

Boat pushed forwa

Path of propeller blade

Water forced backward

Angled blades

Reducing friction

When a wheel turns around, friction slows it down. Friction occurs between the wheel and the ground, and also between the wheel and its axle. Ball bearings reduce friction between wheels and axles. Like rollers, they cut down the areas in contact with each other. Each bearing is made up of a ring and steel balls.

Ball bearings

Bearings at work
To see how bearings reduce friction, roll a tray over some marbles. It slides over easily.

Air-filled tires
Cars run on pneumatic tires, which are filled with air. They absorb bumps in the road.

Spreading the load
A tractor's tires have a large surface area. This keeps them from sinking in soft ground.

Running on metal
A train's wheels are made of solid metal. An inner flange keeps the wheel on the rail.

Power from water

A turbine is like a propeller that works in reverse. Instead of turning and pushing something, it is pushed, and this makes it turn. Hydroelectric turbines harness the energy of moving water, to generate electricity.

Turbine

High water level

Low water level

Water flow

TURNING IN A CIRCLE

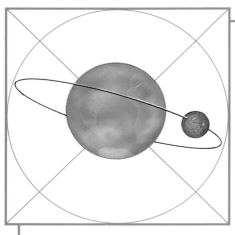

If you tie a weight to a piece of string and whirl the weight around, the string becomes tight. But when you slow down and stop, the string slackens. This is because the weight tries to keep moving in a straight line, while the string makes it change direction. The result is a pull, known as centrifugal force, that seems to work outward from the center of the circle. Once things start to spin, they are also very hard to turn in a new direction. This principle, too, is used in machines.

Washing machines

A washing machine contains a hollow inner drum turned by an electric motor. When the machine is washing, the drum turns slowly, so that the clothes keep tumbling into the water. But when the wash has finished, the drum speeds up, so that it turns several hundred times a minute. Centrifugal force throws the water and clothes outward, and the water escapes through small holes, and is then pumped away.

Heat exchanger

Inner washing drum with holes

Outer drum

Water pump

Electric motor

Drive belt

Lint filter

Amusing turn

When this amusement park ride is still, the chairs hang vertically. But as soon as it gathers speed, the chairs are thrown outward by centrifugal force. The faster the wheel turns, the higher the chairs lift up. A similar thing happens if you swing a bucket containing water.

A steady spin

Something spinning rapidly tends to spin in a constant direction. This is why a spinning coin stays on edge until it slows down and then falls over. A gyroscope works the same way. A heavy wheel spinning on an axle stays so level the gyroscope can balance on a string. In an airplane, gyroscopes show which way the craft is tilting.

Against the curve

When a bicycle races around a curve, centrifugal force tries to keep it moving in a straight line. Without an equal force in the opposite direction, the bike would fall over. This is why you lean over around a curve until gravity equals the centrifugal force. The faster you are going, the more you lean. On a motorbike course, the road is also tilted in to help keep the wheels from slipping out.

Three gyroscopes at right-angles show a plane's angle and direction

Aiming true

A rifle has spiral grooves on the inside of its barrel. As the bullet travels down the barrel, the grooves make it spin very quickly. This spin keeps the bullet moving in a constant direction, although it is still pulled downwards by gravity. A bullet that did not spin could veer off from a straight path. Bigger guns, which fire shells, have spiraled barrels too.

Spiral grooves on inside of barrel

Spinning bullet

GEARS

Like an engine, your body works better at some speeds than at others. If you pedal a bicycle, you will find that one pace suits you best. But it's not always easy to keep to the same pace. If you go up a hill, you cannot help slowing down. If you go down a slope, you tend to speed up. Gears are a way around this problem. They alter the distance that the wheels move when you turn the pedals, so that you can keep pedalling with a fairly constant force.

Pedal power
When you push on a pedal, your muscle power is carried to the back wheel. The pedals are attached to long levers, called cranks, which enable you to turn the front gear wheel with force. Choosing the right gear lets you either increase the force of the back wheel and reduce its movement, or increase its movement and reduce its force. Gears don't give you extra energy, but they make pedalling easier.

Making connections
The chain carries movement to the rear gear wheels. Because it is made of metal, it does not waste any energy through stretching.

Drive chain

Drive wheel

Pedals

Derailleurs
A Derailleur moves the chain from one rear gear to another. A small gear turns the wheel fast; a large one, slowly, but with force.

Fast gear for level or downhill

Slow gear for uphill

Car gears
A car's gear box contains several sets of gear wheels of different sizes and with different numbers of teeth around their edges. The wheels are mounted on two axles and lock together in many different combinations. When the driver changes gears, it changes the way the wheels lock together. Most cars have four or five gears to help control the speed of the car.

Fifth gear
Fifth gear is used when a driver wants the car to go very fast.

First gear
First gear is used when a driver has just started the car and needs a lot of power to get the car moving.

Speeding things up
A grindstone has to turn quickly. Its handle is connected to a large gear with many teeth. This turns a smaller gear, which has fewer teeth. The small gear rotates much faster than the large one. As the wheel gathers speed, it builds up momentum.

Chuck

Teeth that grip drill bit

Bevel gear

Getting a grip
A drill bit is held in place by three metal jaws, which have to grip it very tightly. The jaws are opened or closed by a screw mechanism inside the chuck.

Slow but sure
A rack-and-pinion train has a gear wheel, or pinion, gripping a toothed rack. The train can go up steep slopes without slipping.

Fifth gear

First gear

PUMPS AND PRESSURE

The Earth has a very thick atmosphere which presses against everything on its surface. For example, it presses down on an ordinary chair with a force equivalent to the weight of about 10 people. Fortunately, it also presses upward with an equal force, so the chair stays in one piece. But pressures are not always equal. Many machines squeeze gases or liquids so that their pressure is different from that of their surroundings. Once a substance has been put under pressure like this, it can then be set to work.

Keeping air in

The air inside a bicycle tire is under much greater pressure than the atmosphere outside. But when you pump up the tire, a valve keeps the air inside from rushing out. The valve has a flexible flap or a plunger that is pushed open by high-pressure air from the pump. As soon as you stop pumping, the air inside pushes against the valve, and makes it close.

Air forced into tire

Valve open

Pressurized air inside

Valve shut

High-pressure air from pump

A push from above

When you suck through a straw, you reduce the pressure in your mouth. Atmospheric pressure then drives the drink upward. Pulling up a rubber plunger works through atmospheric pressure the same way.

Drink flows through straw

Atmospheric pressure on drink

Atmospheric pressure on plunger

Reduced pressure inside

Hitting the knob suddenly opens the nozzle to outside air pressure

Pressurized gas expands

Feeder tube

Propellant gas under pressure

Liquid product

Contents forced out of cylinder

Fighting fire

Fire extinguishers use pressurized gas to pump out fluid, foam or powder. When the knob is struck, the gas inside the metal cylinder can expand, and it forces the contents of the cylinder up a tube and out through the nozzle. A similar thing happens when you open a can of soda. The gas suddenly expands, forcing froth out of the can.

Aerosols

An aerosol can works very much like a fire extinguisher. It contains a pressurized gas, or propellant, and a liquid. When you push the cap down, the pressure inside the nozzle is reduced. The propellant expands, forcing the liquid outward. It travels up a narrow nozzle, which makes it break up into very fine spray, like water when you pinch the end of a hose.

Air inlet

Piston

Anvil

Drilling with air

Pneumatic drills work by using air pressure. The air moves a piston inside the drill, and this hits an anvil. After the drill has been used, the air pump, or compressor, speeds up because it tops up the supply of pressurized air ready for the next burst of drilling.

Hydraulic power

If you fill two icing syringes with water (one plunger in; one out) and connect them with a tube, also filled with water, you have a simple hydraulic system. When one syringe is pushed in, the other moves out. This is because liquids cannot be squashed. If you push them out of one place, they have to flow to another. A mechanical excavator uses this principle to force fluid along strong tubes, and the moving fluid operates other pistons.

Hydraulic fluid

Movement in piston

Movement of bucket

Icing syringe

Water in pipe

Icing syringe

LIFTS AND PULLEYS

Everything on the Earth's surface is held in place by gravity. Gravity is actually a very weak force, but because the Earth is enormous, its gravitational pull is very strong. Every time you pick something up, you have to overcome this pull before the object will move. Many devices and machines are designed to help us lift things, or to carry them from one place to another.

Pulley

Rope

Rope

Hook

Pulley

Rope

Pulley

Hook

Pulley

Pulley

Pulley

Rope

Hook

Single pulley
It is easier to pull down than up. A single pulley lets you use your weight to lift something.

Double pulley
In a double pulley, the lower pulley moves only half as far as the rope. But it has more force.

Block and tackle
With a block and tackle, the rope must be pulled a long way to lift the lower pulleys, but they have great force.

Winching a rope
A ship's winch is used to haul ropes, and to pull the ship into its moorings. The winch pulls by friction, rather like a pencil winding string. The rope loops around the winch two or three times, which keeps the rope from slipping.

Scissor grab

A scissor grab uses gravity to grip heavy blocks of stone. When the grab is raised, the weight of the load makes the two arms press inwards. When the load is put down, the grab automatically lets go.

Winding water

An auger is a device that has a long screw thread, which can be used to move something. An Archimedes screw is an auger that raises water. When the handle is turned, pools of water are trapped and slowly lifted upwards. When the water reaches the top, it pours out. This pump was invented over 2,000 years ago.

Arms grip weight

Electromagnet containing a coil of wire

Power supplied by cable

Iron and steel held by magnetic field

Balloon with an electric charge

Mechanical grab

A mechanical grab is used for lifting loose material, like sand or rubble. It has two buckets that swivel on hinges. The grab is lowered with its buckets held apart, then the buckets are brought together like a pair of jaws, so that the grab scoops up a load and holds it. Grabs are operated by cables, or by hydraulic power.

Moving metal

If you rub a balloon against your clothes, you give it an electric charge. The balloon will then attract pieces of paper, and hold them fast. An electromagnet also lifts by electricity. It uses an electric current to make a magnetic field, so that it can pick up scrap metal.

Handle

Tubular case

Spiral screw

Water flows out at top

Water level

Water trapped and lifted by screw

Non-stop digging

A dredger lifts mud from river beds and harbors. It has a large number of buckets, mounted on an endless chain. Each bucket scoops out a load of mud in turn.

Buckets

Transport barge

21

CUTTING

Cutting tools are made from many different materials, to match them to the work that they have to do. Steel is hard enough to cut through paper or wood, but it cannot cut through concrete or rock. For this, blades and drill bits have to be reinforced with other metals, like tungsten, or with pieces of diamond, the hardest known substance.

Combine

At one time, harvesting corn and other grain crops was a slow business. The corn was cut, then the grain was "threshed," or separated from the rest of the plant. Next, the grain was collected, and the leftover straw cleared away. Today, the whole job can be done in a few hours by a combine. The combine gathers the plants with a rotating rake. The stalks are sliced by the cutter bar, and the cut plants travel up into the combine. Here, they are beaten by rotating bars. The grain breaks off and falls through several sieves, while the straw is carried to the back of the machine. When enough grain has been harvested, it is pumped into a truck by an auger (spiral screw).

Straw travels through combine

Rotating rakes

Cutter bar

Grain falls down through sieves

Small teeth

Large teeth

Narrow cut

Wide cut

Short blades widely spaced on chain

Sawing through metal
A hacksaw has a narrow blade with small, very hard teeth. It leaves a narrow cut.

Sawing through wood
Wood saws have large teeth bent sideways. They make a wide cut.

Grain auger

The combine's sieves allow the grains to drop through. The chaff (flakes around the grain) is blown away by a fan.

Mud pumped down through drill

Rotating drill bits

Chain saw
A chain saw has short blades that are angled so that they make a wide cut. The bottom half of the chain travels toward the engine, so that the saw pulls away from the operator and digs into the wood.

Cutting in a circle
A drill is a rotating cutting blade. Only the tip does any cutting. In a wood drill, the spirals work like an auger, and carry away the sawdust. In an oil drill, waste rock is carried away by mud pumped up the drill.

Tunneling machines
Road and rail tunnels are built with giant cutting machines. At the front is the cutter head, a large disk with hard teeth. This head is pushed forward by hydraulic rams, and it slowly rotates, cutting the rock. The loose rock falls through gaps in the cutter.

Waste rock carried away

Hydraulic rams

Cutter head

Conveyor belt

HEATING THINGS UP

Everybody knows what heats feels like. But what exactly is it? The answer is pure energy. If something is warm, its atoms have a lot of energy, and they hurtle about very quickly. But if it is cold, they have less energy, and they move only slowly. Heat always flows in one direction. It travels from things that are warmer to things that are cooler. Many machines produce heat and then pass it on, so that it warms up something else.

Instant heat

An instant gas water heater is designed to provide hot water almost as soon as a tap is turned on. The water travels through a heat exchanger, which is a system of pipes connected to metal sheets. The sheets have a large surface area, so they can collect heat from the gas flames rapidly, and carry it to the water.

Heat from electricity

When an electric current flows through a conductor, it generates heat. An electric kettle uses this to boil water. As the water heats, it forms steam which flows past a thermostat. When the water boils, the thermostat switches off the current. An electric kettle is very efficient; almost all the energy it uses is passed on to the water as heat.

Flue outlet and inlet

Heat exchanger

Combustion chamber

Hot water inlet

Gas inlet

Thermostat

Kettle

Cold water inlet

Water molecules agitated

Element heats up

Heating element

Rotating reflector

Microwave beam

Microwave beam

Vibrating water molecules

Heating with waves

Ordinary ovens heat the air around food, so that the food warms up. A microwave oven makes waves of radiation, which are reflected onto the food by fan-like blades of metal. The waves travel through the food, its water molecules vibrate, producing a hot meal in seconds.

Held by heat

When a rivet is heated, it expands and is hammered into place in metal plates. As it cools and contracts, it pulls the plates together.

Acetylene

Oxygen

Water

Carbon dioxide

Thermostats

A thermostat responds to heat by turning something on or off. Many contain a strip made of two metals. As the strip warms up, the metals expand by different amounts, so the strip changes shape. This movement operates a switch.

Bimetallic strip is curved at high temperatures

Electrical contacts held apart

Bimetallic strip is straight at low temperatures

Electrical contacts meet

Making metal melt

Many chemical reactions produce heat. The flame on a welder's torch is hot enough to melt metal. Its intense heat is produced by a chemical reaction in which acetylene is burned in pure oxygen, to produce water and carbon dioxide. Other fuels, like coal or oil, produce less heat.

COOLING DOWN

Heat can be useful, but sometimes it can be a problem. It cannot be made to disappear, but it can be encouraged to flow away. This is exactly what many machines and devices are designed to do. Fans and cooling fins work by giving heat a chance to escape. Refrigerators and air conditioners work by using heat to evaporate a special liquid. The vapor that this creates carries the heat with it, and when it turns back into a liquid once more, it gives up the heat. By using this principle, refrigerators and air conditioners move heat from one place to another.

Air conditioning

An air conditioner works by sucking in warm air from a room, and blowing it over an evaporator. The evaporator is kept cold by a compressor, in the same way as in a refrigerator. The cooled air is then filtered before being blown back into the room.

Outside air intake

Fan

Cold evaporator

Room air cooled

Thermostat

Insulating lining

Liquid turns into a vapor, and takes in heat

Vapor gives off heat as it turns into a liquid

Compressor squeezes vapor to turn it into a liquid

Moving heat

A refrigerator's icebox is surrounded by pipes, containing a liquid that evaporates to form a vapor. This takes in heat. The vapor is then pumped through pipes outside the refrigerator, and squeezed so that it condenses. The vapor turns to liquid again, and loses heat.

Drill bit

Cooling fan

Blowing heat away

The motor in an electric drill generates a lot of heat, particularly when it is working hard. If the heat builds up, it can melt the drill's wiring. To prevent this happening, the drill has a built-in fan. The fan blows air over the drill, and the air warms up, carrying away some of the drill's heat. Many electrical machines are cooled by fans.

Letting heat escape

Heat escapes more quickly from a large surface than from a small one. The fins on a motorcycle engine use this principle to keep the engine cool. They conduct heat away from the cylinder, and lose it by warming the surrounding air. The faster the motorcycle moves, the more air is blown through the fins.

Cooling fins

Air blows through fins

Cooling by air

Some power stations make electricity by blowing steam through turbines. After the steam has been used, it has to be turned back to water again. The steam is cooled by water, and the water is piped through large towers, where it is cooled by a rising current of air. As the air rises, its moisture condenses, and this makes clouds of vapor.

Steam circulates through tower inside pipes

Steam inside the pipes condenses, and returns to power station

Power station

Cold water trickles over pipes, and turns into steam

FLOATING

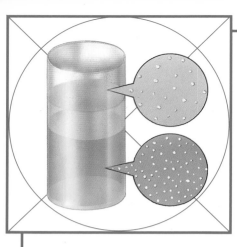

If you pour cooking oil into water, the two liquids don't mix. The oil forms a layer that stays on top. This is an example of flotation. It is caused by a difference in densities, meaning that a given volume of oil is lighter than the same amount of water. Things float in liquids, and in gases. Flotation keeps ships on the surface of the sea, and holds balloons up in the air.

Air outside balloon

Gas inside balloon

At high altitude, the balloon swells up. If fully inflated, it would burst

As the balloon climbs, the outside pressure drops. The gas inside expands

On take-off, the balloon is only partly inflated

Journey through the atmosphere
A high-altitude balloon is filled with helium, a very light gas. The balloon, together with its load, weighs less than the same volume of air at ground level, so it rises.

Full tanker floats low in the water

Empty tanker floats at a higher level

Finding a level
Like a bottle, an oil tanker takes up, or "displaces," its own weight of water. It displaces much more water when it is full, so it floats lower in the water.

Floating and flying
A hydrofoil combines floating and flying. At slow speeds, it floats on its hull. At high speeds, its foils work like wings, producing an upward force called lift.

Hydrofoil produces lift

Boat raised out of water

Buoyancy tanks filled with air

Buoyancy tanks filled with water

Changing density
A submarine can float at any level. It does this by changing its density. It has special tanks that can be filled with water, or with air. When they contain air, the sub is less dense than its surroundings, so it rises. When they are flooded with water, it becomes more dense and sinks.

Pressure of the depths
If you dive underwater, you can feel the water pressing against you. Water pressure increases with depth. A deep-sea research vessel has a reinforced chamber built to withstand pressure equal to many tons.

FLYING AND GLIDING

Birds, planes and helicopters are denser than air, so they cannot stay airborne by floating. They use a force called lift. Lift occurs when air flows over a specially curved surface, called an airfoil. It pushes the airfoil up, and counteracts the downward force of gravity. The strength of lift depends on the shape of the airfoil, and how fast air moves over it. A glider's wings are shaped to produce lift at quite slow speeds.

Streamlined shape reduces drag (friction with air)

Wings at work
Planes that fly at fairly low speeds need a large wing area to generate enough lift. A fighter plane flies faster, so its wing area is less.

In a "swing wing" plane, the wings can change shape, so the amount of lift can be adjusted to match the speed. Wing flaps called ailerons make a plane roll as it turns.

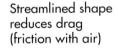

Wing rises — Lift

Gravity

Wing steady — Lift

Gravity

Wing falls

Lift

Gravity

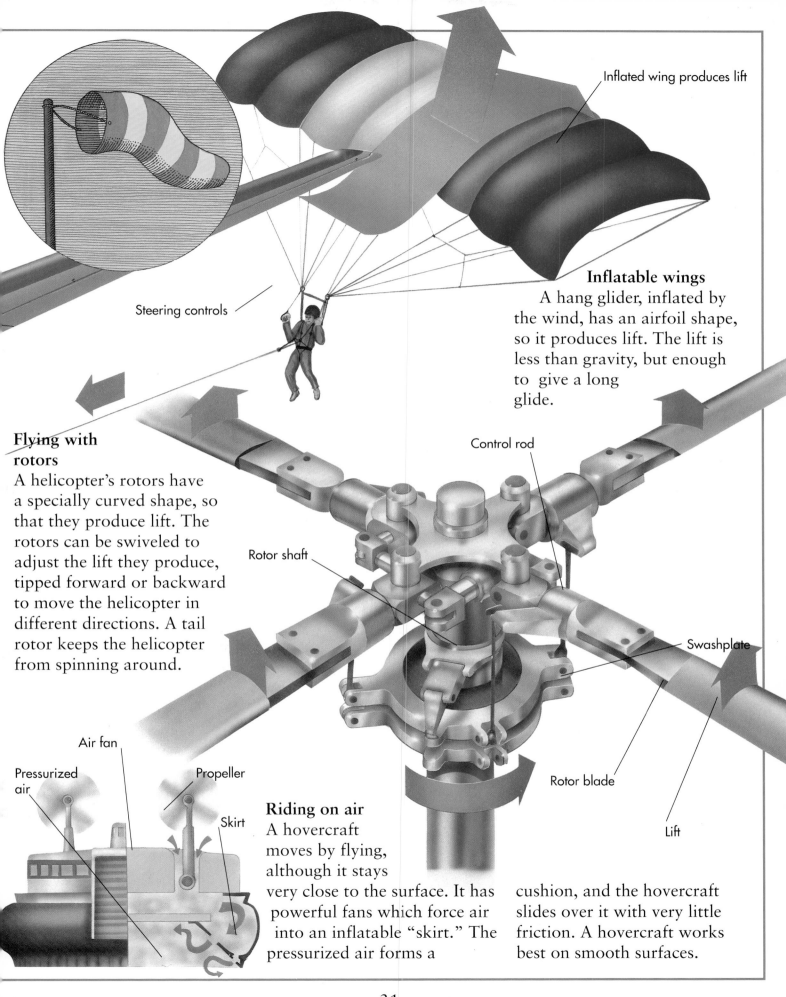

Inflated wing produces lift

Inflatable wings
A hang glider, inflated by the wind, has an airfoil shape, so it produces lift. The lift is less than gravity, but enough to give a long glide.

Steering controls

Control rod

Flying with rotors
A helicopter's rotors have a specially curved shape, so that they produce lift. The rotors can be swiveled to adjust the lift they produce, tipped forward or backward to move the helicopter in different directions. A tail rotor keeps the helicopter from spinning around.

Rotor shaft

Swashplate

Rotor blade

Lift

Air fan

Pressurized air

Propeller

Skirt

Riding on air
A hovercraft moves by flying, although it stays very close to the surface. It has powerful fans which force air into an inflatable "skirt." The pressurized air forms a cushion, and the hovercraft slides over it with very little friction. A hovercraft works best on smooth surfaces.

31

MEASURING

Without help, humans are surprisingly bad at measuring things. It's very difficult for us to guess the exact time or temperature, and hard to judge speed or distance. Accurate measurements may not seem that important in everyday life, but they are vital for machines. Machine parts have to be made to precise sizes, so that they fit together exactly. Many machines, from ships to aircraft, need exact information about the time, and the conditions around them.

Measuring pressure

A barometer measures the pressure of the atmosphere, which indicates the weather to come. An aneroid barometer contains a metal capsule that has had the air pumped out of it. The sides of the capsule are held apart by a spring. As the air pressure changes, the capsule's sides move in or out moving a needle on a dial.

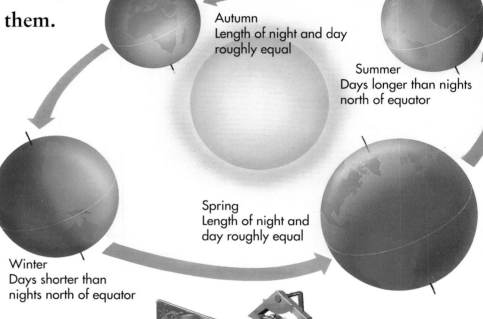

Autumn
Length of night and day roughly equal

Summer
Days longer than nights north of equator

Spring
Length of night and day roughly equal

Winter
Days shorter than nights north of equator

Escapement controls speed of gear wheels

Arm attached to spring

Vacuum capsule

Hairspring

Rocking bar

Measuring time

To measure time, a clock has to contain something that moves at a very exact rate. In clockwork clocks, this is either a swinging pendulum, or a spring that turns first one way, and then another. Modern clocks work electronically, vibrating quartz crystals at a precise frequency.

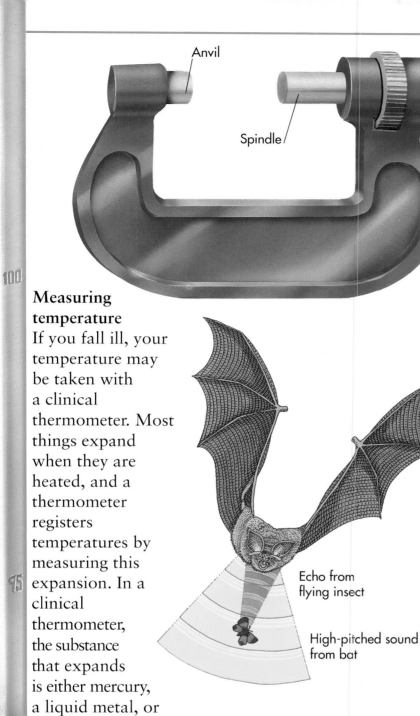

Anvil

Spindle

Vernier scale

Measuring temperature

If you fall ill, your temperature may be taken with a clinical thermometer. Most things expand when they are heated, and a thermometer registers temperatures by measuring this expansion. In a clinical thermometer, the substance that expands is either mercury, a liquid metal, or alcohol. At one end of the thermometer is a small bulb that contains the liquid. When the liquid is warmed by your body's heat, it expands and pushes up a tube connected to the bulb. The hotter you are, the further it travels.

Echo from flying insect

High-pitched sound from bat

Measuring something small

A micrometer is designed to measure the size of small objects with great accuracy. The object is held between the spindle and the anvil. The barrel is then turned, and this moves the spindle forward on a screw thread. When the object is held tight, its size can be read on the gauge. A special "Vernier scale" counts fractions of a turn.

Measuring length

Our ancestors measured distances with knotted string. Today, an electronic tape measure does this more quickly and accurately. It sends out a beam of high-pitched sound, which bounces back from an object, and the device measures how long it takes to do this. It can then work out the object's distance. Bats use a similar system to detect flying insects.

Measuring speed

A speedometer shows how fast a car's wheels are turning. Mechanical speedometers do this by using the wheel to turn a cable. The cable spins a magnet, which drags a drum, and the drum turns the needle. Electronic speedometers work by producing a pulse of electricity when the wheel turns.

Hairspring

Rotating magnet

Needle

STORING ENERGY

A battery is a package of stored energy. When you switch on a flashlight, the battery drives an electric current through the bulb, and the energy in the current is converted into light and heat. Batteries are just one way of storing energy. Machines with moving parts often store energy by winding up a spring, or by turning a flywheel. The amount of useful energy that these devices give out is less than the amount that is put in, as some energy is lost as heat.

Positive terminal

Diluted sulfuric acid

Negative terminal

Manganese dioxide and carbon

Carbon rod connected to negative terminal at base

Individual cell, containing a set of plates

Lead plates

Ammonium chloride paste

Car battery
A car battery has several sets of lead plates in diluted sulfuric acid. As the battery is charged, electricity flows into it. This drives a chemical reaction, which leaves the "positive" set of plates coated with oxide. As the battery is used, this is reversed, and electrical energy is given out.

Flashlight battery
Unlike a car battery, a flashlight battery does not use a liquid, so it is known as a "dry cell." It contains a carbon rod, surrounded by a mix of manganese dioxide and carbon. Outside this is a paste, with ammonium chloride, which conducts electricity. The whole battery is surrounded by a zinc case. When the battery is used, the ammonium chloride reacts with the zinc, which loses electrons, while the carbon rod gains them.

Normally, this reaction would produce bubbles of hydrogen, which could make the battery explode. But the manganese and carbon act as a "depolarizer," preventing the hydrogen from forming. The voltage of a battery depends on the materials used. This one is about 1.5 volts.

Watch battery

A watch battery is also a "dry cell," with layers of mercury oxide and powdered zinc, separated by a substance that conducts electricity. Electrons travel from the zinc to the mercury oxide, creating an electrical difference between them of about 1.35 volts.

Zinc case connected to positive terminal at top of battery

Energy in springs

If you stretch an elastic band and then let go, it will return to its original size. If you bend a thin strip of metal with a gentle pressure, it will spring back. These are both examples of "elasticity." When an elastic object is squeezed or stretched, it stores energy.

The spinning flywheel

You can charge up some toy cars by rolling them along the ground. This sets a flywheel inside spinning, which drives the car along.

Flywheel of toy car

Direction of travel

It releases the energy when it regains its original shape. Springs are designed to store lots of energy in this way. They are made of strong steel to withstand a lot of winding or stretching without breaking. Springs are not always metal. A bow is a spring that stores energy and then suddenly releases it to fire an arrow.

Storing heat

A thermos flask stores energy by making it difficult for heat to get out. It has two layers of glass, separated by a space with very little air. Heat cannot flow through here, as there are very few atoms to conduct it. The flask also has a shiny inside surface. This reflects heat rays, and helps keep heat from escaping.

Insulated stopper

Vacuum

Glass with metallic coating

USING SOUND

If you hold a ruler on the edge of a table, and then give the free end a flick, it will make a sound. Sound is a series of vibrations that pass through air. The ruler makes air vibrate by moving up and down, and the faster it moves, the higher is the sound's pitch. Lots of machines make sound, and although they are more complicated than a ruler, they work in much the same way. They have parts that vibrate either at a fixed speed, or at one that can be varied.

Electric bell

An electric bell contains three main parts—a bell, a coil of wire, and a metal striker with a springy arm. When the bell is switched on, electricity flows through the coil. This creates a strong magnetic field, which pulls the striker toward it. But as the striker moves toward the coil, it breaks the electric circuit. The magnetic field disappears, and so the striker moves back to its original position. This completes the circuit again, so the sequence of movements starts once more. The striker's rapid action makes the bell ring.

Bell

Switch

Battery

Coil wound around
iron core produces a
magnetic field when
current flows through it

Springy striker arm

Contact made or broken
here

Metal
striker

Sensing with sound

Sound travels even faster in water than it does in air. An echo sounder, or sonar, probes the sea by sending out bursts of sound, and then timing how long they take to return.

Floating objects, like fish, reflect the sound sooner than the ocean floor beneath them. Dolphins use high-pitched sound to locate food, just as bats do in air.

Sound waves from ship

Sound waves

Echoes from fish

Echoes from fish

Sound waves

Megaphone

Making yourself heard

Sound waves spread outward from your mouth when you shout. By focusing these waves more narrowly, a megaphone makes you sound louder.

Loudspeakers

In a loudspeaker, a coil of wire is wrapped around the base of the speaker funnel inside a circular magnet. Electric signals passing through the coil create a changing magnetic field, making the funnel vibrate.

Circular magnet

Base of funnel surrounded by wire coil

Cardboard funnel

Air blow out

Stator

Air sucked in

Electric motor

Rotor vane

Sounding the alarm

One way to make sound is to "cut" air with something sharp, so it starts to vibrate. Woodwind instruments work in this way, and so does a siren. A siren is made of two parts—an outer stator, or stationary ring, and a moving rotor. When the rotor turns, its vanes sweep past holes in the stator and blow air through them. This makes the air vibrate, creating a noise.

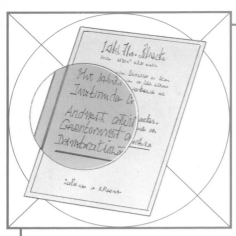

USING LIGHT

Light energy travels in waves. It always moves in straight lines, but it can be bounced by mirrors and bent by lenses. Most of the things around you do not make any light themselves, but reflect light made by other objects, like the Sun or electric lightbulbs. When you look at something, your eyes take in light and use it to form an "image," or picture, of the object.

Focusing motor

Lens

Diaphragm alters amount of light entering camera

Semi-silvered mirror reflects part of the light to viewfinder

Incoming light

Autofocus camera
Cameras take in light, and focus it onto a film. The film records the pattern of light, and this is "developed" to produce a photograph. Many modern cameras focus their lenses automatically. The incoming light is reflected by two mirrors. One sends light to the viewfinder, and the other sends it to an electronic microchip, which focuses the lens.

Muscles that change shape of lens

Vitreous humor (jelly-like substance)

Nerve leading to brain

Cornea

Lens changes shape to focus light on retina

Iris alters amount of light entering eye

Retina (curved screen containing light-sensitive cells)

Making things bigger

A compound microscope shines light upward through an object on a slide. The objective lenses form a magnified image of the object inside the barrel of the microscope. The eyepiece lenses then work like a magnifying glass to make the image about 500 times bigger.

Eye

Eyepiece lens

Objective lens

Mirror

Focusing knob

Second prism reflects light backward

First prism reflects light forward

Eyepiece lens

Sliding tubes allow image to be focused

Incoming light

First mirror

Light bent through 90°

Second mirror

Bringing things closer

Telescopes and binoculars work in the same way, but binoculars save space by using prisms to reflect the light. The lenses gather light, and then bend it in sharply. This makes the view seem bigger.

Looking around corners

Looking in a mirror, you see things back-to-front. But if you look around corners with a periscope, they are the right way around. A periscope has two mirrors. The first reverses light rays, the second puts them back the right way.

Cutting by light

Daylight is a jumble of wavelengths, but laser light has just one wavelength. All the waves move in step.

Waves of ordinary light

Waves of laser light

SENDING SIGNALS

In 1888, Heinrich Hertz discovered radio waves, an invisible form of energy that travels at the speed of light. People soon found that radio waves could be interrupted or altered to make them carry signals across distances without any wires or cables being needed. Today, our planet is bristling with radio waves of many different lengths, or frequencies. Some carry signals that radios convert into sounds. Others carry signals that TV sets build into pictures.

Making a picture

A television collects radio signals and uses them to trigger three electron guns which make the screen give off light. The guns send out electrons, which are bent by magnetic coils where they strike the screen in just the right places at the right time. If you look closely at a television picture, you will see that it is made up of tiny strips of red, green and blue. A special mask makes sure that each beam lights up strips of just one color, and together the colors form the picture. The screen makes a new picture 50 times every second. The pictures are still, but so close together they seem to move.

Glass screen

Electron beams

Shadow mask with holes

Strips of 3 colors

Electron guns —one for each color

The compound eye of an insect produces an image made of many points of light—just like a television

Satellite communications

Radio waves usually travel in straight lines, although they can be bent and reflected by different layers in the atmosphere. A satellite collects radio waves from a transmitter on the ground, and then reflects them back over a wide area. The reflected waves are collected by a special parabolic dish, which focuses them on to a receiver.

From signals to sound

A radio aerial responds to radio waves by producing a weak electrical signal. The radio amplifies the signal so that it is strong enough to drive a loudspeaker (p. 36). Radio waves arrive almost instantly, traveling at the speed of light (about 185,000 mph).

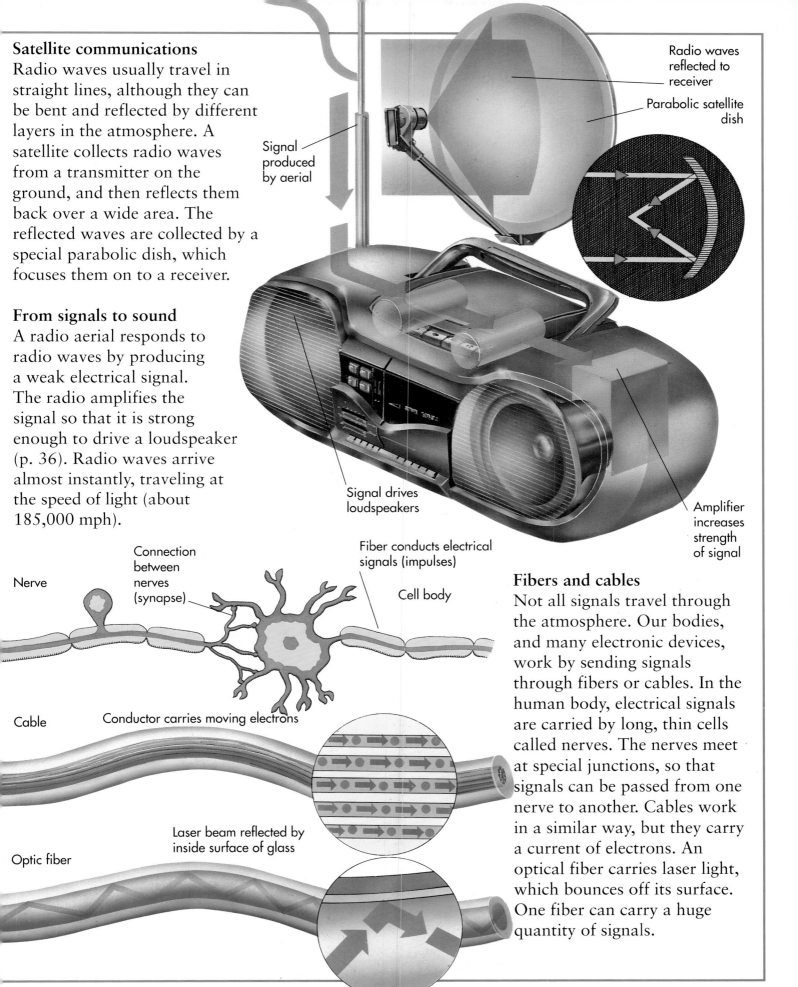

Radio waves reflected to receiver

Parabolic satellite dish

Signal produced by aerial

Signal drives loudspeakers

Amplifier increases strength of signal

Nerve

Connection between nerves (synapse)

Fiber conducts electrical signals (impulses)

Cell body

Cable

Conductor carries moving electrons

Optic fiber

Laser beam reflected by inside surface of glass

Fibers and cables

Not all signals travel through the atmosphere. Our bodies, and many electronic devices, work by sending signals through fibers or cables. In the human body, electrical signals are carried by long, thin cells called nerves. The nerves meet at special junctions, so that signals can be passed from one nerve to another. Cables work in a similar way, but they carry a current of electrons. An optical fiber carries laser light, which bounces off its surface. One fiber can carry a huge quantity of signals.

MEMORY MACHINES

Information is something that we use all the time. The words in this book contain information, as do pictures, computer programs, and even pieces of music. Storing words or pictures on a page is quite easy, although it takes up quite a lot of space. Electronic machines store information in a much more compact way, either by using magnetism or by using light. At the touch of a button, the machine converts the information into a form that we can understand.

Magnetic tapes

A tape is a ribbon of plastic with a magnetic coating. Sound recorded on a tape converts into electrical signals. These are sent to an electromagnet, which magnetizes particles on the tape. When the tape plays, the particles create a current, amplified to produce the sound.

Analog and digital

In an analog tape recording, the information is stored as a continuous stream of magnetism, which varies in step with the signal. But in a digital tape recording, the information is stored as millions of separate patches of magnetism. The patches work like a code, and the machine "reads" the code to make the sounds or pictures. Digital recordings give a very clear sound, because the code is very precise.

Cassette case

Tape with magnetized surface layer

Guide wheel

Record/play head

Drive pillar pulls tape through player

Analog recording

Varying magnetic field

Patch of magnetism

Digital recording

Compact disk

A compact disk player is a digital machine. Instead of storing information by magnetism, it stores it as a series of microscopic pits. As the disk spins around, a laser beam shines onto its lower surface. The beam detects the sequence of pits, and the player uses this information to assemble a sound or picture. To play just 1 minute of music, the player reads and decodes a sequence of over 2 million pits. The pits also hold other information. This enables the player to check that it is working properly, and allows it to locate individual tracks.

Computer disk

Areas of magnetism on disk

Read/write head moved by electric motor

Floppy disk

A floppy disk is a form of magnetic storage used by computers. It works like a tape, but instead of winding the disk back and forth to get to a piece of information, the computer can move across the disk to reach any point. This is called "random access." It allows the computer to handle information fast. The computer divides the disk into separate sectors. It keeps a record of what is in each one, so it can quickly move its read/write head to the right place.

Direction of disk

Credit cards

The black strip on the back of a credit card holds details, like an account number, in magnetic form. When the card is put in a machine, it reads this information.

Credit card with magnetic strip

Strips marking code

Close-up of underside of a compact disk, showing pits

Tiny pits create a color pattern, like the scales on a butterfly's wing

Beam reflected by pits on disk

Laser

Beam passes back through mirror

Photodiode detects the laser beam

Semi-reflecting mirror sends beam to disk

9 780749 60703 6

Bar codes

A bar code is a group of numbers that can be read using light reflected from a laser. Thick and thin strips make up each number.

43

THINKING MACHINES

A computer can be "programmed" to carry out many different tasks. It can even monitor itself as it works. At the heart of a computer is an intricate system of tiny electronic circuits, packed into components called "microchips." Pulses of electricity travel through a microchip, carrying information which can be stored, processed, or used to make something move in action.

Computer signals

A computer works in the same way as your brain, using electrical signals. Computers have only two kinds of signal —"on" or "off." These are used to build up larger "binary" numbers. A binary number can stand for all kinds of information, from a letter in a word to a dot in a picture. Computers process information by carrying out binary calculations at great speed.

The brain

Eyes and ears take in information from the outside world

Muscles make the body move

Electric motors make precise movements

Bones provide something rigid for the muscles to pull against

Hydraulic pistons provide power

Metal framework

A computer works by representing numbers with "on" or "off" signals

An abacus works by representing numbers with beads

0101 + 1000

OFF ON OFF ON   ON OFF OFF OFF
5   8

= 1101

ON ON OFF ON

13

Robots

A robot works rather like the human body. Its muscles are electric motors or hydraulic pistons, and its brain is a computer. Robots and humans differ in a vital way: unlike a human, a robot can only follow its instructions (program).

Computer controls the movements of the robot

Computer peripherals

The chips in a computer take in electrical signals, process them, and then give them out. To be useful, they have to be connected to devices called peripherals. There are two kinds of peripherals. Input peripherals create signals and send them to the computer, while output peripherals take signals from the computer and set them to work. A keyboard and a mouse are two examples of input peripherals. They convert the movements of your hands into signals that the computer can understand. Monitors and printers are output peripherals. They convert signals into images on a screen or words on a page. A disk drive works as an input and output peripheral, according to whether it is taking in signals or giving them out.

Monitor (output)

Mouse (input)

Computer

Keyboard (input)

Printer (output)

Disk drive (input/output)

Address line

No pulse stored = 0

No current in data line

Pulse stored = 1

Computer programs

A computer program is a long list of instructions, written in a form that a computer can understand. Each step is very simple, but the computer can perform complicated tasks by carrying out millions of steps a second. A program is loaded from a disc into a chip called a Random Access Memory (RAM). The chip contains huge numbers of tiny switches, each of which stores one of the "on" or "off" pulses that make up the program.

INDEX